What Is Severe Weather?

by Jennifer Boothroyd

first step nonfiction

Lerner Publications Company · Minneapolis

LERNER

SOURCE™

Expand learning beyond the printed book. Download free, complementary educational resources for this book from our website, www.lerneresource.com.

The images in this book are used with the permission of:© ollo/iStock/Thinkstock, p. 4; © Sven Klaschik/iStock/Thinkstock, p. 5; © iStockphoto.com/javiagm, p. 6;© Jim Reed/SuperStock, p. 7; © Purestock/Thinkstock, p. 8; © Clint Spencer/iStock/Thinkstock, p. 9; © Comstock/Stockbyte/ Thinkstock, p. 10; © iStockphoto.com/DelmasLehman, p. 11; Courtesy of the National Oceanic and Atmospheric Administration Central Library Photo Collection, p. 12, 22; © Purestock/ Thinkstock, p. 13; © Stocktreck Images/Thinkstock, p. 14; © Mayra Pau/iStock/Thinkstock, p. 15; © WhitcombeRD/iStock/Thinkstock, p. 16; © Jorgen Udvang/iStock/Thinkstock, p. 17; © Michal Bryc/iStock/Thinkstock, p. 18; © Maxim_Khuar/iStock/Thinkstock, p. 19; © pjgs/iStock/Thinkstock, p. 20; © Mark Hayes/iStock/Thinkstock, p. 21.

Front Cover: © Minterva Studio/Shutterstock.com

Main body text set in ITC Avant Garde Gothic Std Medium 21/25.
Typeface provided by Adobe Systems.

Lerner Publications Company
A division of Lerner Publishing Group, Inc.
241 First Avenue North
Minneapolis, MN 55401 USA

For reading levels and more information, look up this title at www.lernerbooks.com.

Library of Congress Cataloging-in-Publication Data

The Cataloging-in-Publication Data for *What Is Severe Weather?* is on file at the Library of Congress.
ISBN: 978–1–4677–3919–1 (LB)
ISBN: 978–1–4677–4682–3 (EB)

Manufactured in the United States of America
1 – CG – 7/15/14

Table of Contents

Thunderstorms

Look at those clouds. A **severe** storm is coming.

A **thunderstorm** brings lots
of rain and wind.

5

A lightning bolt lights up the sky.

Lightning flashes in the sky. Thunder booms loudly.

Scientists study weather so they can warn us when storms are coming.

Scientists study thunderstorms.

Thunderstorms happen all around the United States.

Stay indoors during a thunderstorm.

This cloud is a **tornado**.

This is called a
funnel cloud.

A tornado has strong
spinning winds.

Tornadoes can cause a lot of damage.

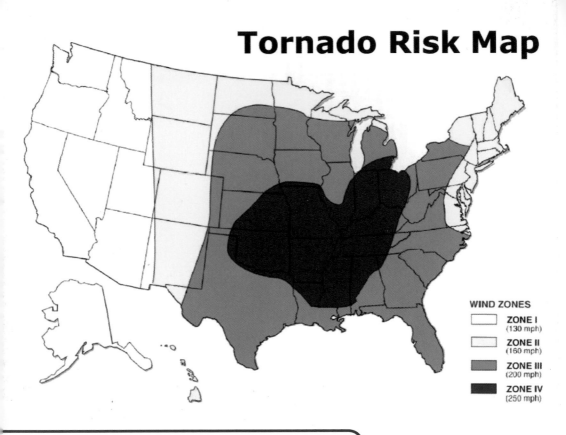

Tornado Risk Map

WIND ZONES

- ZONE I (130 mph)
- ZONE II (160 mph)
- ZONE III (200 mph)
- ZONE IV (250 mph)

The states that get the most tornadoes are colored in red.

Tornadoes have happened in most states.

Stay away from windows during tornadoes.

Go to a building's lowest level if there is a tornado.

Hurricanes start over the Atlantic Ocean.

These storms have heavy
rain. They have very strong
winds. 15

A hurricane moves closer to land.

Hurricanes happen on land close to the ocean.

Water covers this street after a hurricane.

Too much rain can cause a **flood**.

Signs show the way to leave this area.

Many people leave before a hurricane hits land.

Blizzards are winter storms.

Blizzards have lots of snow and wind.

It is best to stay
inside in a blizzard.

It is hard to see outside in a blizzard.

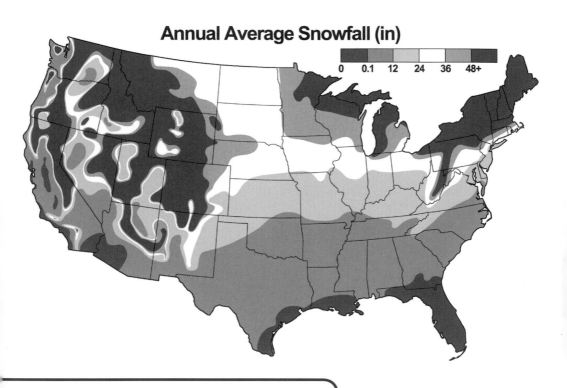

Annual Average Snowfall (in)

0   0.1   12   24   36   48+

The areas that get the most snow are colored in dark purple. Does a lot of snow fall where you live?

Blizzards happen in areas that get snow.

Glossary

blizzards – severe snowstorms with very strong winds

flood – a lot of water on usually dry land

hurricanes – storms with very heavy rain and very strong winds

severe – very strong and serious

thunderstorm – heavy rain, thunder, and lightning

tornado – a severe storm with dangerous spinning winds in a funnel cloud

Index